Other works by the Author

Bound for Roque Island: *Sailing Maine and the World*
Bound for Cape Horn: *Skills for Expedition Cruising*
Offshore: *Collected poems 1969 - 2020*

The Telluride Murder Mystery Series:

Gatsby's Last Resort
The Fat Man

Cape Horn 2007

Offshore

Offshore

R. J. Rubadeau

R. J. Rubadeau Books
Beacon Hill Publishers, LLC
Books That Matter
Durango, Colorado
rjrubadeaubooks@gmail.com

LIBRARY OF CONGRESS CATALOGING IN PUBLICATION DATA:
Rubadeau, Robert John, 1948-
Offshore
1. Title
ISBN 9780981731339
ISBN 9780981731339

In order to be a sailor, you have to go to sea.

Peter Pye

For

M.

Pitcairn Island 1974

CONTENTS

Part One

A PIECE OF WORK

Ondine /Tasman Sea 1974

FOXY'S
Jost Van Dyke, B.V.I. 1974

It is good fortune to have a woman around at drinking time
two is better
whispering, trilling, ashen words with purgatory intensity
they eye me with shifty smirks
pull at their bright tight halters, expose patches of skin, uncaring nipples
ignoring me time after time
with attention
this fading island twilight deserves.

a dutch name on a tricksters beach,
stainless drums against a plywood board,
a black guitar and a wife who knows the two
watches,
amused at the curtain drama
of a beach, a sunset, a mix of amber angst
around the tortured neck of a twelve-ounce bottle of beer.

studying the light
the two women,
Foxy,
with eyes tightly shut against the next song,
a chicken wanders through
bound for the edge of grass beyond the slivered moon of sand
I think of Boston sleet, dirty slush, slow death
times of despair, rude drivers
nights of stinking humid radiator warmth, mindless talk radio.

of the two birds
the blacker one speaks first, with bright teeth, pink tongue, ruby lips and obsidian eyes
chinning the stars, around a well used toothpick,
insulted that I hadn't bought them a drink, yet
the sun in retreat spots the renegade chicken, Foxy's wife worries it with a glance,
and disappears in green foliage quickly
with out
so much
as a by your beehive.
have you ever slept in the solid, cold sand with coconut crabs nibbling your ear

BOUND FOR ROQUE

Telluride, Colorado 2004
Winner of the Mark Fischer Literary Prize 2004

water is two parts hydrogen
oxygen one, Lawrence said,
a third thing makes it water,
                    and no one knows what it is.

sly, willful, molder of granite
hiding as bergs or airs in temperature
they carve atoms for pleasure and fail yet to define water
moving as fluid.

we muggle in
sated opinions of water sold by those who go to the edge and dive in
just to get wet.
when I found the sea I was barely eighteen, knowing it was never a home
to be infected with delight.

ghouls of dead sailors share late dog watches on sleepless nights
tugging at kelp laden anchors off rocky lee shores
a hundred hissing yards away
waves boil in sibilant gibes of sweet cruises taken or drowned at birth by
children
pissing in long arcs off the teak deck with both hands shroud bound.

bound for, never
going to,
a reality of voyaging
vexing surely for land bred owners on a schedule yawping at the yacht
club bar.

in my log book I put bound for Roque,
a place with bamboo fog and cold black Fundy tides
failure is only in never leaving port.

NEPTUNE'S CAR
Damarriscotta, Maine 2002

skin peeling wind tugs at torn tarps broiling over
a fetched wooden stern
waving with open seams to miles past
with scars of paint feathers and
oakum spills in trills of cotton caulking falling like
blond curls on a lass who shouldn't torture the boys
but can't help it
any more, again
she's seen the hard toil of better days
churning slowly, making way under
a square of canvas muling
against the tide, tugging along sideways with the wind in her
hundred year dreams
of Liverpool, Biddeford, Le Harve
and the strangled creeks of a thousand other bean towns
unloading shoe leathers
slate, bodkins, dead trees,
oily black coal.
the men who ran her
tumbled her
like a well used whore
daily put shoes to her
stubbed her with hot ends of fags
spoke only in sibilant oaths
called her names
cracked her spine
stuffed her full and by
spit with the wind on her deck
forgot she was a ship.

twice a day now the tides suck her soggy timbers, mussels and barnacles clean as she leans against her butt sagging sisters waiting for the day in a short while when a change takes place in the eyes of bridge front walkers and small business squeakers of ice cream and fancy coffee going in a heartbeat from leaning chintz relic to eyesore and the chainsaws will roar and the century of life service will go away forever on the anything but sweet mud banks of the Sheepscot River.

CALLALOO SOUP

Hope Town, 1972

a'buy me, say she
we hungry all right say we
head bob, do she
wait we fine by the sea
patiently
open now maybe
Jus-now, she be softly say
cutting dasheen smartly
by machete,
bocca man scraffle on by
the dusty way
don't bounce me, no good, surely
he soca sway
wait we, for christophene, bake-up cakes, and callaloo soup.

NAKED DOORS

Hadley Harbor, Elizabeth Islands, Mass. 1985

in the no contest zone
between dusk and dark
dinner gone, mansion house dark, Grant's ten chimney tomb, lit,
dinghy george and me rowing on mirrors all alone
with her sheer fullness always in my sight
portholes in orange, mast tips oval the sky
dishes clanging, sodden sounds sulky in the metal sink.

kids on deck
aping from the mizzen shrouds in lazing half loops
the horses neigh
the gulls whine
night falls with the certainty of blackie's bean soup
oars drag in silent balanced drapes
into the cold waters as the stars open up endlessly all around the treetops.

tonight we'll make love
silently, almost
a naked door separates us from the tossing
deaf ears
of sleeping children, damp sheets, tangled feet
in quarter berths growing too small too soon under an open hatch
by half.

love sighs tumble from
our mouths,
slavering tongues
knees on pillows, stolen inches
narrow slot berths, perfect for twined limbs
made longer in
strangled shouts of quiet jolting joy.

the boat giggles
at our sweet torture
remembering maybe
a half century of such
things,
that love does
for want of
nothing else.

CAT GUT BLUES

100 miles East of Freeport, Bahamas 1974

Snipping, bleeding
separating
squeezing
tugging, tweezing
pulling the cat guy sinew
of double ought stitches
from my face.

bracing,
swaying certain
berating
the mirror for holding
still never
while the boat meets
the swells of the Sargasso Sea.

where horses died
out of kindness
starved of water
in the swirling holds
of the cesspool sump
in the center of the North Atlantic.

I watch the tears drown in my brown eyes
with each pull
and think of all
the tears I never cried
for all the reasons I never tried to save a horse
and thought again, what a barren thing
being bound out on another delivery, late before we start, always is.

you held my free hand when I put them in
pulled it to your chest, looked behind the water on my cheeks
to tell me I was brave, stupid, brave
but all I heard
was the bark of the laugh
you gave the doctor when he said I couldn't go to sea
until he took the stitches out

LISTENING TO THE DAY
Cabo San Lucas, 1974

first full awake brutalizes the senses on a drool damp bunk pillow
leaving dirt smell and rut passion behind in check of a grab at your briefs
light swarming through restless portholes
dancing in hot globs against the teak and holly sole
feet caked in fire ant salt
crystals invading puckered crevices of tender sun-strained skin
smells of yeast, stale woolen socks, monkey fur, gingivitis.

on your back now swaying against the hull
gurgles, hollow tocks of waves slap,
taps of bare feet in the cockpit fighting the last sleepy miles,
a giddy headed red haired woman hides behind closed eyelids
you beg for a tumble
into sleep where she waits with waffle slats on her thighs
from creamy beach chairs and lonely fruit drinks slathered in sweat.

a higher groan leads the discordant melody,
blocks under stress creaking in harmony
tanging lines in loose lipped bundles riding in sine up the mast
a tugging jib rippling along the leach with a lisp
a base line of hobby horsing water tonning along the line
random beat of a target zoning on the radar with a muted squeak,
a loose can romping among the artichokes.

bells yet rung
no hurry to boots
rolling along bowlegged
water hot kettle
skin drying cool
eyes gunked open
seat cover bungeed up.

listen to me
watch time
spent time.

FRENCH MOUTHS
Brest, France 1977

weighing specks of Breton dust in the window shafted sunlight
pushing puddles of blood red wine around the wooden tabletop
listening to faces we can't, won't see
smelling gaulloise
stinking of burning carrion
sweet tar, garlic
french mouths in lopsided twists.

looks kill neutral nods
constipation is not an expression
to show a stranger
to be used lightly
disdain, disappointment
dis-everything,
approval
the harbor stinks with consumptive floating élan.

staccato attacks
sounds of scratching bird shits, corn mouths
rattling fans, phlegm
manhood questioned with horned finger jabs
we drink with purpose in the growing dark,
ready to swig, hit, and run
from wooden handled folding knives,
gifts of their fathers.

why they are so angry
why they are so brutal to give us Piaf
breedings, lost scowling jowels, pusses on faces
centuries of truffles,
snails, fish eyes
and bad temper,
pardon
we.

BLOWING HARD ACROSS THE BAR

San Juan, PR, 1979

blowing hard
across the bar
hands spread
to a mahogany wheel
in baritone
the waves grow as a well hooked fish story.

he had been there
he said
where spew flew
groaning marching beards breath
a steady bassoon
of doom and deep soggy death.

his stories rehearsed
eyes shifting under white brows
a smile behind thin mottled lips
always
he was
the last left standing.

I bought a drink
his thin frame shuddered
as the grease found a home
in his throat
a hunch of thin shoulders for pay
met.

the Puerto Rico Trench is 16,000 feet deep
he said,
pausing
where would he go
from here
I wondered curiously,
I needn't have.

TRACES OF OXEN BLUES
San Francisco, 1998

the work of a boat is
as common as mud
give me those
who hook on the gang
plank on plank
to approach the thing
as an empty bottle seeks
a down island full proof rum.

take away thrill, romance, self
sweat down the thing
hunker the water weary leagues
in long steady
bouts of claustrophobic certainty
from one horizon to the sameness next.

stubborn boats beat, pounding
the toiling pompous
ass of miles,
those who
skirt the outside expecting clarity
mistake the meaning of moving water
for soulful endeavor.

bang down the night dram
on words
that swing gimbaled with white froth, courage, weather worse,
blue nails,
give me limericks
hoisting and working oaths
tunes, bawdy, ill kept, dirty
piss hard grit helps the endless moment move.

sailors who go
to sea for poetry,
killing the poor thing
for life,
but for them, bard, on a cosmic journey
we are caught explaining
water to fish.

THE GREEN FLASH
Unalakleet, Alaska 1981

in the bright blue twilight
that went on hesitating
hopeless, reprieving, against the short brutal night
the sun slid dolphin style
towards the sea, towards
the north pole.

fire crackled, smoke swept away
good clean arctic air, as
children ran sideways along the beach
racing sol over drift wood logs,
Yukon born burls, whorls in gray lopsided circles
fuel, warm, squeals and puppies, heads in laps.

queering the thing
yapping about rarity
admitting it might be a hoax
the smell of blood and moose whispered
from a stew pot of DNA
we waited.

eyes clicked the last tipping orb
horizon violet in blue
knowing it was already in Siberia
with friends and vodka, black sturgeon
eggs in sacks
stink meat and dried flipper sewn tight and buried, spring treats.

the flash of green froze
us
all saw the shriek of color, hushed,
frightened in portent,
tsunami washed, the fluid flushed to our feet at the edge of the Bering
Sea
the only time, ever
except for the rest.

we hugged our kids,
talked in clouded whispers
shared things forgotten, lost, frozen, sipped with dry mouths.

HOLES

Gloucester, Mass. 1982

by necessity holes are in something
it's one or the other
making everything you thought
you were and less, accountable
by the exception
opening below when expectation
laws, physics, integrity, lags.

a liter is less, imperial,
terror begins with less, when
water is two miles deep and
tons of lead are wanting
to rest
on more.

air leaves like a cheerleader heading for the team bus
after a game, full of bounce,
and skirts a flutter
while you wait for your mother
her Pontiac
to drive the point home.

a bottom is not really always down,
it is
said a ship will tumble in free
fall on its way to a watery grave, do we
lose
hold
be
for
the
end

PREDICTING THE PAST

Hell's Gate, Saba 1986

voyages often begin in the last moments of ending badly
working your way south
in endless swells
of slicked back skull locked greasy hair and hail
good cheer when all
you really want is for the waves to flatten out.

searching for that one cloud among the rest
anviled on the bottom
as if the horizon
was razor wire
against the escape
of over shooting the mark.

edgy sleep, anxious skipper
tins of cold food
cautious wombs
of tangled hope
and smiles that should hide
behind the last time you wished for a happy ending.

you dream of two men
carrying slop in a two handled bucket
from a restaurant up cobblestones, milky
smells of any one awful thing
other
than salt, and reeking fear of a soundless drop to the ocean floor.

endings happen
in energy expended while new
starts linger in
struggle to find the strange clarity
before dream blink open eyes
and the clanking mind engages like a black belching cog railway on palm green hills.

are all red eyed unsolid mornings dust locked
in land bound yearning
where houses don't shake,
with a dirty lust for brown roads groaning ahead under slate plate
cowered skies
until you finally find
what you never.

El Fin del Mundo 2007

A LOVE POEM AT SEA

100 miles Southeast of Portland, Maine 1986

the wind came in from two thousand miles away
to tousle your tangled salt sprayed hair
stretched out in the cockpit
eyes squirting out the puckish sunrise
after a long
watch in silent idle
waiting for the stars to evaporate slower than the horizon and give
us a sight.

the kids forward
safe
inking the night sighs back
to a space
when
alone was our blessing
and all others
cursed for intrusions.

salt cakes the eye corners, slits of soul green
in small feet
of cautious crows, lovely smiles
as the smooth years run under the keel
in the stuff we feel
for all the juicy
growing
together.

just another dot and a circle
on the landless chart
spilling over the table
representing the lusty oceans
tumbling sex
endless picnics
open air frolic
of our life.

SCOOTERS IN PARADISE

The St. George Dinghy Club, Bermuda 1970

Gibbs Hill lights
the onion patch
under
oleander, waifs, glasses of slick, while
wind burgles past pink
walls of stoned roads
all twisted and sic.

a pinder rushes past
St. David's Head lights
by jagged kitchen shoals
on a course east of south
in yellow scarves and white gloves to scabby elbows,
nose hair and waddles.

Hamilton plays tunes
St. George in asexual harmony, discordant yeses
lost past Somers Island drowned in
Sea Venture 1609
dogs with more noses, shorts with tight cumber buns and hairy legs,
manic mooching manners of all sorts.

her chin on my shoulder
crotch to rump horsepower
breath of jasmine
skin dry as perch
good
night was nipped, rooted, slobber.

on the back of a scooter
rum punched in skidded
road rash of prime colored flowers
before the tide took us south
to brutal expectations in the trenches,
triangles.

CHANGI BEACH
Singapore, 1973

hair to here
end of line for cut rate postage,
voided smiles
cleaner
police in teak polished batons
herding thinks to the scummy water's edge.

boat's people
junks in cans
living, cooking, laughing
smelling of oiled chili, tapas
bamboo rushes
the bus to Changi

home of five cent coffee
boats to island worlds, hiding in between nets on the beach
mangroves, tangled roots
of people in rags happy to be
separate, long time, long time, mister
so, so say simply.

red ant lines, nipon bayonets
starched, crushed, impoverished grass
peacocks, white table cloths
mallets of skinny wood
resting
in cabanas of cool lace hats.

beaded curtain shops
chuff chuffs, yellow Mercedes buses
diesel stinking sails on barges
heading into pirate waters
lives stunted shut
in Lord Jim apologies.

CREWS

Tasman Sea, 1974

sail boys messing
about
coming, apart to
risk a
block exploding, winch bound, mast swimming, keel sucking air,
or left behind
on a dark banshee night in the moonlight.

hours of dismal
same
broken in
seconds of terror
waiting for something
to let go, get loose, head south, get wicked.

two kiwis, an apartheid,
a brit maybe,
the doctor's son
rotating through the days
pushing a dot within a circle
across the square blocks of paper oceans.

waking the off watch
trolling for sharks on lines, sheets, gut checking over two miles of gurgle,
tempting each ear
with stories, wishes
dreams
of boats, women, drunks, and
low down salacious lies.

no questions, asked
every, single, foolish, thing,
taken as fact, almost
heartfelt
respect in the
watery halls of the
loquaciously committed.

shipmates are
in mind
fucking
friendship
faithfully full
in vital flickers
passed.

HOMEFREE Sir Francis Drake Channel 2018

CONCH LOVE

Freeport, Bahamas 1976

James was as black as finger nail dirt
Belafonte eyes, sweet torte smile
with a way about him to melt cheese
shirt buttoned open
for the gold he would wear if he could.

slow, proud, left footed, shuffle
cocky in a way you could not see,
eyes rimmed in pearl white, roaming
like a stoned crab.

days on the boat, nights elsewhere
clucking at long legs, bright bound kerchiefs, in
tin sided worlds of fast talking hearts and sweet babies galloofing
in the soft cool light of kerosene wicks.

breezes, jasmine, fronds flacking
roads of black bubbling asphalt,
shoulders of razor grass, ticks,
crawling lizards of love,
lost in the days that move outwards
slugs in lust,
living with a coolness heart
through a vacuum of guiltless banter.

smiling still,
James keeps alive
dreams, in a fresh well,
leaking nourishment
in a hold on a smack with patched cotton sails,
ballooned like a barristers belly
beating back towards Lucaya
ahead of the storm.

MORNING TELLIN

Hope Town, Abacco 2005

she be strolling on sandal soul shoes
sharing sunrise tellin
back bay in morning's time
peaking long slow lazy winks at the life moving
feather heavy, petal hard, lids parting over the yard fence
all day talking, path sweeping
back lane walking girl.

softly shamble on the day
crook'd arm on flopping straw hat
my oh my oh, brown eyes housing
black sheening lightning
talking she is
smelling lime oh, my oh
dreams she talk too true.

house on cat herd land
high ground surety
tumble down tree and mounds of storm
in times she walking
debris of last night, say
when came the dead questions of grainy pictures
when to say family never stay.

but morning she come on fast
and the tall man walk the lane past
two times oh, more, stooped shoulders
looking after her,
always tellin
willing her well on palm tree clacking wind
with shutters propped open and true.

where he go
who he see
that girl may be
better know for once sure
tellin true
on steps street, oh my oh,
she say in whispers to the lonely morning tellin.

SHAKE ME A LEG
Isle of Shoals, 1979

they once sold dolphin penises
as necklace
fetishes
for men looking to women
to save them from drowning.

sailors begged the night
to give them legs
over hammocks
lapis smooth skin without the shrill
tongues of fishwives.

eyes that watch you
rolling on their sides
lolling in bow waves
fixed grins
playmates, harpoon targets, by-catch, dog food.

when I was a fish
fear of dolphins made me sick
the death of speed warps
unimaginable by flukes and Boston flakes
I called friends.

now I put my belly to the teak deck
and stare back, knowing
what I know
being what I am
not alone.

LYING TO TELL A MORE PERFECT TRUTH
Kingstown, Saint Vincent 1976

do I
envy the swagger
of owners in their parade
on the squeak and holly floors
of high powered racing machines
bitching the time slipping towards the line
cursing the wind backing away from the goal
torturing the heartbeats spent doing anything else.

sit quietly,
count the hours in the log
marveling at the arrogance
of biting black flies
moving with a condescending dare from a waving backhand
tempting you serious
in a swat to find
nothing but naval dust.

keeping peace
on the tongue
in spite of dangerous
mistakes
yet to happen
to you
to them
to her.

watches are full of manly voices
tales of clear escape
stories heard in endless
conviction of the rightness
of decisions that change the counting world
in a matter of speaking inside the circle
that puts the fingernails to the blackboard
in hot bunks across an ocean.

black flies always
jump backwards
before they fly
and scooping them up
holding them clenched
and banging them in an overhand throw
against the bulkhead
feels right.

after the lines
in the bars
at the clubs
along the streets
smiles of good fortune
even from the losers
who never learned to
fly without jumping first.

to tell them anything
to hear them say
a thanks
as true as
a lap dancer's first name,
makes all the swatting
cribbing, gnawing, disliking
worthwhile.

BLUE PETER

Padanaram, Mass. 1996

the boat closes in around me, a ratty favorite blanket
days go and come again in late summer, hot
in languid chains
nothing ends or begins, sea breeze sighs
moments of sweet indolence
spread like thumbtacks on deck to keep Patagonians at bay.

driven to move by tightening sinew
I row away
heading no where but distant
each oar stroke a furrow in my soul
soon
I scuttle back, climb over the rail, hurry below
lay back down.

chores pock mark a lonely afternoon
watching others
anchor, leave, grab moorings
one tries to speak
sees my face and clams shut
with a furtive look at her mate,
they give us a wide berth.

finally the oars take me to the dock
strange, thumping feet
chatter, frozen smiles, ice blocks
garbage bins, aluminum rolling carts painted red
lined up to make it easy
to come and go,
why?

I see her out heaving in the pack
underneath a ghostly blue flag
P
peter
like a blue sky
ordering me back
aboard,
all right.

DEATH MASKS

Naushon Island, Mass. New Year's Day 2000

as many rooms as centuries
on this day to mark the thousandth celebration
of the thousandth celebration of the count down, count up
red wine sipping around tight cheer
fireplaces in many corners of huge rooms
where president's dawdled
Grantlike, Clintonesque, Cleveland ledged.

rooms lead to stairs to closed doors
to wings flying in random corridors from everywhere
sheep graze in rock fenced splendor
the winds of Buzzards Bay gnarl trees in ceaseless
roiling toil to find the northwest coast of Labrador
two track trails canopied under old growth elm
leaves to shins in dirty cold water puddles.

sailing a twelve and a half
into the new thousand
in gusty guffaws
with sweet friends
bobalink docked
under tender mackereled skies
in cold chill toasting a brand spanking time.

that night the middle teens
opened the lids on
death masks
of the ghosts, bound tight
in cedar chests and tissue papers,
we tried to explain the need,
failed wickedly to raise the hackles of the jaded MTV generation.

later, screams, of nerves, as dark replaced trained pixels,
razor edges of sleep
kept
the stairs creaking
shutters banging, oil lamps burning
until breakfast swept away the magic
in a cold nor'easter to cross the hole of a new millennium.

MISTER FEAR

52 degrees south, Pacific Ocean 1974

it is mister fear
not some weak simpering sister of miss scared
terror is sponge-cake
horror is scalded kitten milk
fright is fleeting bat wings
doom sounds rhapsodic when hulls oilcan between viselike grumblers.

skulking in dark horizons under scud headed clouds
cracks of phosphorous lightening
flying battery acid ripping flesh from bone
humming shrouded wails just below hear level
rattering leeches, shotgun reef ends
flushing cold green water over high boot tops.

mister fear puckers
confuses, coyote like
panders
snivels, lies
cheats
stretches time without an oasis,
wins over every miracle.

there is no cure
no bargaining
no quarter
given
taken, cool, less
tears wrenched
judged severe, gaveled.

mister fear
is undying, heartless with sharp little gold filled teeth
and open gasping jaws
of surrender
in crawling bunks
and hugged floorboards
when hell is all loose
and land a wedding memory.

HOLDS

Wye River, Chesapeake Bay 1992

tilley, teflon, tiller, ties, tape, taylor, twists, turnbuckles
radio, rolls, rigging, rings, rod, roe, rope, roil, rouleau, rust
salve, sails, sand, saw, schoon, scull, shackle, shad, shank
needle, nave, noodle, node, nipple, nook, nut, nymph
fedora, ferule, fichu, file, fin, flake, flag, flatware, flax, fleece, flesh
jar, joke, jerkin, joint, joggle, junk, juice, jejunum, jersey
dodo, dodger, dowel, dram, davit, damp, dagger, danseuse, distributor

the place where it all ends
up side to side to side
holding the bottom down
necessary as measles
useful as regrets
tidy as worms in a tobacco can.

below the roots
above the water table
stuff finds itself, mating, breeding
yet never offers a clue
to what
you really need
when.

accumulation is rampant
growing to fill each void
most never sees the light of day, again
most never finds its reason for being
there,
now you know
the tricks and deceits of spares.

ALONE IN THE GUN HOUSE
English Harbor, Antigua 1979

the zipper on my sea bag
won't shut
so I can't look
for a berth today

curtains flutter
in sea beam catenaries
while hibiscus fuzz claws
its way through the dead cat smell between my legs

morning tease
in plate silver lead pitchers, cools
squirmy milk reminds
you of all things dead sometimes
move again

the silver chain from the loo is hanging
men
talking in the sea shell street
while the horn rimmed trades
pounding
tell me
I've stayed too short.

ALBATROSS
Pacific Ocean, 1973

I needed someone to lash me to the shrouds
as the mountains crept up from the sea
blue in swirls of clouds that we saw coming
rooting the longest silent wail from my guts
in fifty-days the sirens worked their spells
poking my belly in a bloating sickening stream
charging soul crushing wants named only
when demons chased albatross flying in
lurping lines over forty feet of swell, forty south and a half
chasing unnamed stories of turtles and stone heads, lost souls
on the current, easting towards an island that never wants the dead
left and sought again in dismal need for
burgers and cable above the keening cry of poor locals
I walked through the skin of a mirror and lied
shamelessly in a constant moaning of need
less holy by far than a stone headed god and his bloody angels
of today's tumbled explanations.

Part Two

RUNNING WITH THE TIDE

Ondine Pacific Ocean 1974

YOU SAT THE BAR

Lucaya, Grand Bahama Island 1976

you sat the bar
challenging me to be the next
guy you would blame
for all of it.

swizzling
in tight red lips
and black eyes of lacquered lashes
over the rim of chipped glass.

crossing legs
exposing calves, clefs
bleating snatches of dark
quisling shadows under a red hammer flowered shift.

hard promise, chrome heart
pink nails, creased brow, boiled knuckles
with a dance card
of a well
used spittoon.

thinking what it might have been, mussed,
days after in a sweaty bunk,
tasting the last grueling beer on the ocean swell
and the casting off,
smelling lost islands of sweet hibiscus, blue wet and horned eel grass.

DARK ENERGY

Mesa Verde, New Mexico 2004

ashore, now
pushing apart, drifting, unconnected
in matters physicist don't dare dream
of women in no clothes, blue plated eyes, sterile attitudes,
challenged,
studded tongues,
stars that don't shine, black holes that won't close.

over half of the stuff in the universe isn't
people crying in crumpled rubble, shit on their face, bullet
holed
craters in walls, fifty caliber truths
earth thinks of the cosmos in its own terms with hilarious tragic
results
or, at least the ninety-nine percent of us who were born here.

five billion years, the way things are going, until the Big Rip
everything going away from everything in its own direction,
bound for nowhere at the speed of light
exploding novas will save us in a healing fireball in half the
time.

dark energy is seventy percent of everything,
and it's getting stronger.

ROWING

Tarpaulin Cove, Naushon Island, Mass. 1990

one clapping hand
Socrates and Limbaugh debating a rubber chicken is nothing
necessity in fact,
compared to the cosmic futility of a one oared dinghy in a crowded
harbor.

rowing is arcane, torture
some profound metaphor it is probably not
simple ergo-mechanics for the trusting rower
backwards towards your bow is a good idea, but
hard sell on a busy city street, sometime.

pull right go left
push right go right, pull left go right
pull both oars and the boat arcs out in a huge lazy circle bound to circle
back to
          where you began
a greased hockey puck, everything usually makes it worse.

fending off is an emergency procedure that requires spinning around,
dropping the oars, standing up, scooting forward, using your precious
hands to get
          between two colliding objects
scooting forward changes the velocity, your hands push air while the
boats greet each other, clunk
nothing but what you are pushing against to hold you up.

my children take it seriously
as long as I am watching
best practices is a pre-adolescent needing to be rid of parental space
as a floating Alcatraz, to leave the herd pen you must row
lessons become pie to instruct motivated learners.

Tarpaulin Cove
I vant to be alone
get arrested, I snap back at my daughter,
my own hoped for outcome of aloneness means divide four by two
in chronological order, horses, sand, abandoned lighthouse, life
preservers

pulling like starving castaways, they flee towards the only space in sight
all muscle, no technique, my son sits in the stern holding on tight, acting
the mute bosun.

lecherous laughing, I frown at the flailing oars,
libido comes leaping out of hibernation aboard as the tots beeline
in fits and starts,
churning a froth for the sweet soft foam rolling at the tide's edge
how often in cruising does one thing lead to another and another after all
rowing is a central part of the grand scheme.

Dog Star /Jewel Island Maine 2016

FRONTAL PASSAGE

Gulf of St Lawrence, 1969

it looks so dark
the end of the world is off the horizon, just over
six flat miles away
wind coming on, owning it
teàring away at the cool gray calm
shattering morning hopes
of easy times, timely arrival.

waterspouts twist and turn
weaving between clouds and churn
waves dance slamming
banging black boards of screech
running toilets of viscous flu
bucking backs of granite gargoyles
until it gets worse.

pressed down
pumped out
waiting,
straining in cold shivers
watching hope fade
in other eyes,
teeth grinding, wind and wave mounting, from behind, intrusively.

childhood sanctuaries
lost, forgotten
needed, fondled,
with head down, turning away
to keep wind and spit inside our teeth
shortness, breath in chests
too little to scream.

a slap of sunlight
a rising of the hull
past, gone, without
a single word
hauling around, cleaning
up
thanks forgotten, as it scuds into the past towards Sable Island.

BONE FACE

Fort de France, Martinique 1976

carnival sparks
through the streets
with white flour
flung with just a
hint of spite by
black faces
painted skull boned white.

gray sewage
flows in gooey currents
through the anchorage,
chunks of
processed
French sauces, garne
crabs, unwashed greens, condoms, dead fish.

waiters wait
outside dark ochre doors
in matched white coats
with gloves
smiles cemented
ready to light with sharp incisors
if we pass through the door.

all day, all night
parades pound through cobblestone streets
as wrought iron balconies
swell with those who find
less to their liking
than sinless rituals
in masks to save faces already boned over.

SKIN LIKE IRON
Pitcairn Island, 1974

I want to wear my skin like iron
I want to do right but not right now
I want to plan on miracles
I want to know tomorrow's weather
I want to never decide to not go again and be wrong
all is welcome on Pitcairn.

Christian gave me a grass skirt
and his sister
to dance with under old scratched records
of drums, tin roofs
and thrums
in a house with breadfruit, linouleum and stringy chicken
shark teeth set in ebony sea drift trees.

songs of sailors
in open boats under tall cliffs
and skiffs bedded on land with
dead men lining shallow black caves
women leaving all behind to be with the four
who died one after the other,
tidy scaffolds for ones who turned back at the brink.

bounty burned to a watery grave last
anchor in the town oblong while
two kids swing with Christian
and all the snakes that don't
belong in paradise
with mail we brought over five thousand miles
from the weak chinned kiwi queen.

iron skin would let me
look
and
not
see the sameness of every day and
imagine that the love is
what matters
in paradise.

COWARDS

Gloucester, Mass. 1971

there is a tearless coward hiding in each of our hearts
stowed away, quiet, furtive, guileful
you see others in plain sight, embarrassed
denying your own at soul peril
hoping the lid stays on
the keel stays down, the pointy parts up.

pan, pan, pan
shilling imminent distress
about you
signals a presence
just off camera, always just off,
corner eyed shadow, gloomy gus
wading on back bending spindly legs in the shallows.

jibe first, throw it over
lay a trail of floaters
clawing back, upwind
letting hope trickle in
doubts boil, stream a piss mate
crew names screamed a-quiet among the noise.

shaken,
hiding the gutless treason
soggen next steps forward
to retrieve
all that was vainly thrown
away in the first
anguished holes of fear.

S.O.R.C
Ft. Lauderdale, 1972.

ball banging testosterone
clanging
down the dock with
donkey testicles dragging straining sacks
over spidery dock lines
past ass ends
of branded machines
vowing to never
see them again.

loud, deep
bassoons
full of hale, chilly, backwater
humor
and boat names
of convictions, snide
lessons in life,
aggression, tenacious, hot kiss
war baby
tension, condor, yankee girl, till.

young empty heads and old gams
as it ever was
as it ever was
full of stuffing
nervous to fail
eager to be on stage beneath the chute
scudding
before the gulf stream
sorts it all out.

strangely
I always feel suddenly sadder at finish lines
even when I am the first to find it
no two are ever the same
no smile
no triumph
no finger gesture
is ever worth the end of something.

SEA TIME ALONE

The Gulf Stream, alone 1976

I only have a single black specked petrel
to think with today
others have tall humping waves, voices, nerves in smoky tendrils on
greasy green slopes
others have anvil clouds leaking in an upside down sky
envy a wing
dive bombing troughs, tripping on spew.

a fly spends an hour spinning my mind,
ten thousand progeny
from a single fruit
miracles with faceted eyes on a varnished grate
an erection from somewhere
leaves melancholy behind after lunch.

dark masses of trees,
howler monkeys, macaws, leopards, shrill in their colors
cast their mazes before me in the darkest morning hours
only to erase the din the next moment
struggling with ton laden eyes
over slippery sea-sucking sounds,
they drown,
smelling on the dying wind
the decaying roots of palm sized spiders in paper thin jungle soil.

feeling the world tip surely towards the sun
black and blue horizons
tumbling, bottomless pits of deep trench endings
dawns extinguish sightless sounds with dangerous sleep
winks one as the booming guns, distant and safe, rumble
in a hurry to hide,
sea blackened rocks, inscrutable, humble, lonely
as solitary backgammon players at dusk
in amongst the howler's trees.

at lunch
erection back, comfortably
tiller in hand, I worry that
another day will never come
again.

NEWPORT MONDAY MORNING PAPER

Newport, Rhode Island 2003

the first seaside crime of the morning hit
the mawing pit in my stomach, tightened the screws
grew cat whiskers, and died goofy,
I asked Digger for another jorum of skee.

Winchells in tight wooden kimonos howling their well paid yaps
buttoned, off the nut, on the fade, ringed in the wet from my glass of nip
shnozzled all in a dither from the headlines, on the bar with Mona Mars,
the girlfriend, drifting a dutch with a Buick thrown in for the extra war
time presses.

morning bar mirrors behind mahogany tinted bones nurture silly grifter
lies
Bogart, Hammett, Raft showed us the way a lip should squawk
with no beholding ankle, exclusive as a mailbox
short on the geetus, with faces built for radio.

stop again with the roscoes I say to the by-line
leave the little frail out of it,
pull in that droopy mug or I'll pop a tooth into next week,
imagine
black ink newspaper rants as thin as a hoofer's wallet and
cold as a toad's belly.

gunsels and eel juice, kicking the gong around in Bahgdad
zotzed, ribbed up on Texas gravy
to skate around the truth with a gasper hangin' from my lower lip
while the stiff I am to meet today is busy getting undressed for work,
this peachy morning under the butcher's thumb
everything's jakeloo.

FREE PRACTIQUE
Martinique, 1977

question, query, queer
quibble
quid, quiver
quirk, quell, queasy
quiz.

each time I ask for admittance
I admit I expect to be rejected,
who in their tolerance would let me in
when keeping me out makes so much sense,
yet they do, I do, we do.

quarry, quiet, queue
quinine, quiver
quota
quintessence
quack.

languages merge into smiles, frowns
eyebrows raised,
scowls, wide eyes, winks, tsks,
hands moving, pens sliding in grease across the page
money changing,
hands again,
slapping foreheads,
warnings in words no one understands.

qualm, quake
quip
quite, quotient
quit.

the first step ashore full of one time expectation
fresh juice, cold beer
glass plates,
din of strange words
voices in back rooms around flickering screens
pushing the rest of the world back to sea
without you.

NETS ON THE BEACH

Deshayes, Guadalupe 1976

every time I point to the sea
he spits at his feet
head down, missing
blessing the blood
of god, I guess
mumbling into his white beard bastard
French.

I squat in the sand
trying to get under his brows
my accent worse than
his finally gave it up
looking over my head
out to the ocean's
deadly edge.

eyes palest
reflecting blue on sickly white in bleached black sockets
holding
nights of heart and bone terror
lurching days of all the misses
near or not to the fish,
gnarled hands in the net for a moment unpredictably quiet.

the boat he sits on, worn green with
bright yellow gunnels,
flat, dangerously flat, wormed wood
sweeping to bows that climbed no sea
spared no wave, wooden locks, warped oars
open, exposed, leaking
twisted as the rope handle on the old bucket under the bows.

every day into night he takes down his net,
spread in flakey black strangled folds on the driftwood sticks
leaves the sand
dies a little in the darkness
to feed his well
of lost life
measured in fish eyes.

pourquoi,
I ask.
who can say
he answers in fine English
as he waves me away
I do
that night I eat lamb stew in wine mottled wonder at born luck
on the balcony over the street.

Dog Star/Roque island 2013

TIDBITS

Manchester Harbor, Mass. 1999

suicide to stay
murder to leave
what would you do

birthdays come, equator transits
hang another on the line
pearls strung in swine muck

ocean rules
before me you swam the sea
before you I would too

nothing left to loose
after free to be cast off
me, ghosts and the boat

jutting land
doubling masses
challenges taken all over again

sails full
and by, drawing
aloft, alone, aloof

land people from the sea
look on stage
living lives in dreary contest

engines run
when they will
despite creative oaths of persuasion

45 degrees north 35 degrees west
waypoint Weld, first tried
I wish he never died

fickling winds come
from all wheres
boxing a compass of life.

VOODOO TIDES

Baie du Carenage, Martiniqe 1978

vodun, she spat wetly fire around blood red lips
showing the lines in her gnarled palms, standing knee deep in scummy salt water
always a part of us, she whispered in a volcano voice
throat open, older than the world
swaying, barking, writhing in sensual chest born groans
her black head spinning in sheets
stronger than dirt while
adepts drum a heart.

baobab trees
spitting chickens in flames
dried heads
snake, monkey, owl, you
elephant tongue
changing destiny
one midnight at a time.

botono, sorcerer, witch
offering dark bo
to the stringy night
false gods fly true on veined gossamer wings,
steps as light as moonbeams on a cobweb
she doesn't talk to, but becomes
god.

ancestors wander in silent witness
horns blaring
returning again in a swaying morris mini
to dance with spirits
alive
cursed
to live, on
until the question stops being asked.

SOGGEN SPIRITS
Coogee Beach, NSW Australia 1973

how do you call a ghost
hey, ghost
in fluid, all swirled together in sea graves
not alone in dirt
should it be
easier, less, troubled, hard.

Slocum had his
Portuguese sailor
steering a rhumb line
strung out on plums
lost at sea
the first man, and a foreign ghost
could he be mine, please.

voices heard in the shrieking wind
needed, heeded, lost
thousands at the horn
Hatteras, Lizard
Sable Island
where horses share
the deep, frisian sands.

if ashes count
Weld, Chichester
Jones
my father
whispers of chants, not mouthed
form on late bells, early horizons
breaking loose from the dark sea at dawn.

when my spirit does come is there a sex?
does the choice follow
tried and honor or mischief self
will steering help,
is life stretched out on a fish line
pulling along in a frothed wake of those ahead.

I hope so.

DOUBLING HEADLANDS, FORELANDS, BILLS
Beaufort, North Carolina 1997

in the forenoon we doubled
the Horn
boldly,
evocatively
pitching seas crowing at having lastly, drakely
reached,
rounded the last place left from nowhere.

Cape Wraith,
Scotland's only,
Cape Clear
Fastnet's goal,
Hatteras
tomorrow waits to pounce in graveyard light,
Cape Cod mews
dunes swept lonely by pilgrim's blight.

Bloody Foreland
in Ireland's noggin, a low place of scraggled houses
Mackish Mountains against the sky
flat topped with steep slopping ends tobogganing to the sea
green escapes with golden fringed
beaches to hide the bones
of Belfast's own.

the tide race of Portland Bill
ripping in channel bores
hopes bank on a single biscuit toss from shore
Lyme Bay stretches fifty miles away
Wallsend of the sea
only,
fools and boyos go further.

Lizard Head light beams the Atlantic
leading to Falmouth and the start of it all
chips sponging grease in upside down paper hats
cherry faced girls arm in arm banging smacking
red lips together
shops on slopes, stones a kilter
harborland stenchy, cheeky in reserve.

not worthy of the rest
points are dimes plus change in dozens
Conception breaks the angels warm and leaves the cold
Punta Gallinas, Punta Malla, Point Hope
leave lives in their wake,
crying all be mine.

the basaltic columns of Port Davy
cathedrals of druid hue
thundering waves from the southern ocean
pound the knees off
Bass Straight fishermen, holding
Tasmanian eyes searching for poisoning safety of Maatsuyker Island
endless elevators of thirty feet tumbles in blue ocean silk.

not all headlands are like that
some benign, deadly
one side bright,
dark side differently woven
all in a space of shrapnel time severing imaginary lines on the water,
closing a circle
full circle
opened by going out and around.

SHED GRIEF

Admiralty Bay, Bequia 1973

in the dark, far up beach
by the metal shed, humming in the trades
feet shuffle
as the palms clack
on this night
of waiting
and loss.

momma cries softly
looking over deh bay
a brother, a son, lover, man, any
way, she cries softly
no spoken asides
weeping
for the run, too often, shamelessly, rutty.

t'Vincent
winston, ganja, and beer
we wait, for a groaning sound beyond the reef
knowing it is long past late
gone, she say, surety
in a flat
bottomed skiff
skidding to the bottom in blue myth.

all for fun, serving the want
a night of
haze, heroes lost
and crying on the jungle beach
for the gone
one
more sea life
tasted.

DESPACHO

Mona Passage, Dominican Republic, 1996

bulls charging on washborn skids
lightning holds no dark relief
thunder no silence
Luperon of the mangoves in switch back bliss
away beyond
stakes of green
and red tape night time arrivals.

in bound from the shallows of the north
despacho in hand
nothing serves to dry an eye
calm a nerve
shelter a naked mast on
a night squall line
in Mona Passage.

owners quake in cabins
away from metal plates
alone at a glance, huddled
in risk of meeting a skylight dagger
hissing of strikes near the rail, above the wail
of the wind in the rigging
trickles of cold relief down your back.

dark drags through pitching piss
solid water in each breath
choking
shuttered eyes to stay away, awake
reefs, green jumbles, smelling of iodine
waiting for despacho
to get inside.

SAUDADE

Gloucester, Mass. 1969

mornings come stumbling with winsome pangs of wanting to be
some where else people are longing
in ways that bring tears to dead eyes
birds chirp, gulls sqaw and it reminds
me of summer dusk and butterscotch,
slippery rocks and tide scum
pools with scuttling treasures and long skinny legs.

knights of columbus sway at three
keeping their grip on the bar
for one last shot
complaining of the fish
blessing themselves
calling the virgin, mary
for one last shot.

rusted hulls
and two names connected with and
leaking a steady stream
in smelly water
astride the fish dock
hoping for one last go
before november gales end it.

lives should have been
lovely, warmly tongued
young girls swish to school
on the beach
in the cars in the late afternoon
longing for someone
who doesn't know
saudade.

A BILLION YEAR TIFF

Choptank River, Chesapeake Bay 1992

in her belly
nagging treasure
last screams
sobs, child gurgles
bobbles and Inca gold
warm piss from twinkled bladders
secreted in nonchalant blue eyed gazes.

she whispers to me
at night
when no one else
hears the words
just beyond the hiss
and clank of gear on deck
snores, rumbles, tumble homes.

why have you left me
she says each chorus
I am here
always here
you went away, forgot
peevishly, full of nettle
accusing me of personal salty betrayals.

the fury of storms, she whines
despairing calms
playful squalls
bipolar frontal passages are all love, she pouts
torturing the last
painful
excuse for breathing from my lips.

DOCKSIDE

Padanarum, Mass 1980

sitting on the dock
boats every
where
bobbing dreams
callous few, plus more
visually insulting
those of us waiting
wanting
waiting.

scars on the water
lines of scum
growing barnacles
leeching copper, iodine,
poison
longing

tanging lines
popping blocks
pissing pumps
rolling fenders
snatching lines

launch empty
people
less
going no where
feckless

cancer full
scorpio too
crow-winged
black slate night
soul thieves at moorings

a crust is all I need
and some thing
to steer it by

GIBBOUS MOON
SYDNEY, 1973

hiding most of you in darkness
the bright halfness
leads the eyes around
a curve of gentle
nothing
is as it seems,
more.

the boat rocks in irritating
swells from
a storm to the west
opposite the gentle
breeze
winding its way off
the clouded islands.

hollow inside,
leaving again people
known forever
just met
never to see
ever
again.

atolls draw a sadness
of life
bordered in thundering
Pacific waves
and coral so shallow
so bright
it is over in an instant.

moon trails a soon gone path behind
an imaginary line to a wet cheek
good
bye,
is anything
we do so
misnamed.

SHORE TIME
Acapulco, Mexico 1973

I remember the animal dreams
four legs fully planted
on solid foul smelling earth
rooting, snuffling, looking
down the alleys, under doors
of land bound roofings.

the spell was opiatic
felt at once
leaving the water
searching for otherness, closeness
after long weeks in watery climes
crews have no defense, wanted.

swine we become in a twink
filling voids
grunting demands for more
greek sailors eating
any ol' thing the sirens
placed on our plates, in front of our snouts.

spell broken, back at sea
memory lags
stomachs queasy at what
we left ashore
our dignity, a morsal compass
gone, left behind, again.

Part Three

SPIT THE LEE

Patagonia 2005

CUTTYHUNK

Cuttyhunk Island, nine-eleven 2001

tragedy is product bourn of other times
Greek, Phonecians, seppuki
wars of sepia,
Dunkirk, Ohio, Beirut, Berkeley.

spilled bodies in the air
tumbling to empty
streets in chalk dust and
rubble from places in buildings
one should never see,
September one one.

wind, steady,
unfickle, true from the east
moorings tugging at tethered
times when they shouldn't be
held there at all.

wavelength images on the old Bendix direction finder radio, news
casters searching for the right tone
of outrage, despair, moral
poverty of under
standing in ruin

deserted in toasted meringue
crusts of lonely beaches, departed ferries
rusted and tan, beds full of bivalves
in narrow channels of scratching sand and eel grass graves.

the skies clear in the star speckled aftermath of a single day
without a visual reference to mourn under
a bangled banner of innocent, pregnant mothers
fleeing from choked tunnels of dead
cars to Brooklyn.

three days it blew, one
for each plane plus one
radio images searched for lovers, stories as old as Medea, black
slate, pictures in bold
colors of black, white, blood,
wistful hayfields all of green

MARK

Whangarai, New Zealand 1984

he flew for the world to see
up
side
down
in a bi-plane
over the masts in Auckland
under the trestle bridge on the Rangitaki.

leather shoulder straps
stretched against white cracks
buckles of tarnished bronze bending under the strain
wind whipping in shrill tones
laden with tones of death
the engine un-muffled in protest
killing centrifugal force, gravity.

a sheep up at his father's
crop dusting string
of low wing rockets
fifty-five gallon drums of liquid preservative
one hot, still afternoon
waiting for Ondine's engine to groan for the first time since Hobart
we waited, each in turn, for our terror moments in the fume full sky.

two years later,
Newport, learning
Mark was gone
tangled in a wire
at the edge of a crop,
I remember his huge hands, blue eyes, curls close, shy sideways smile
larger than life on the fathom wide wheel at sea, learning
in quiet confidence of twenty somethings peacefully pushing death's
humor.

ON THE HARD

Minnefords, City Island, New York 1972

dream struck, awake
no thing rings
true the deck stays put
the rattles lessen to
gone in the endless, solid
days to hard, on the hard
lost.

making do expenses
beers in the after morning just showing up
to see yard birds
never been to sea
at twice my worth
boggling away at
the defenseless boat.

at sea it is akin to the incidental
random moment when
three waves rise to one
lifts the boat on a pedestal
to admire her belly
swollen in life, choked quiet
to crash back to chaos in a blink.

life's pathways at countless ends
holds the center
of lanquished yard days
in the dampest of wet showers
and the calm
of stiffeling
no airs.

clarity always comes the frozen instant before
the iced trickle at
the neck awakes the fact you are now
sitting in it
coldly, brutal awake moments, solid, predictably
you could not pay to have again when pondering any of life's land bound
decisions.

I FAIL FAIR ON A FISH
Lucaya, Grand Bahama Island 1976

palest
blue green

channel
bound

reef
racked

skipping
lure

sun
sparkles

zinging
hooked

headway
slowed

scramble
astern

strip
line

run
reel

chomp
clean

pressure
gone

wahoo
head

'cuda
fed

SALT WATER CURES
Coogee Beach, NSW, Australia 1974

blue eyes rummy
said he,
salt water cures.

every
thing
finally.

sweat,
tears,
soaking poultice, no need for more.

running away to,
places
dry enough to drown a camel.

immerse your
self
neckly.

poisoned
thing cured
finds a way to your heart endlessly.

like an insult
spoken in cruel smirks by swarthy strangers
you can hear moaning above the wind.

cures
come or not
simply in ways you never imagine.

THIN SLEEP

Sydney-Hobart Race, Bass Straight, Tasmania 1974

skin deep
thin sleep
wet shimmer between
here and over
there among jungle creatures
chattering along the borderline.

plowing the way
running it down
wedging the heaving ocean apart
slipping through darkness, dayness
left with a cozy caress and a kind slap
seldom shown to full bodied women.

conversations on deck
in your head alongside
her and there,
watching a bead of cool freshwater sweat naked
rolling down her ambered lanquid
vase-shaped
glass.

no time for abandoned, gone over slumber
when Yaeger voices
strain their cool
wide eyes along the rods
bending and stretching stainless life
to bands, rubberized, tortured
in ways no life line should be.

sleep comes skinny
in pounding rhythms
in working ways to windward
off watch
worried
frightened constant
of no one thing in particular.

THE HOLE IN THE WORLD

48 ' 30" South 125' 30" West, 1974

In the southern ocean at about 48' 30" south 125' 30" west you can find a place called the Hole that lies about sixteen hundred miles equidistant from Pitcairn Island to the north, Cape Horn to the east, New Zealand to the west, and Antarctica to the south. Aside from a few astronauts and their moon orbits it is the single place on earth where you are the farthest away from another human being possible.

do souls have a place they go for space
to know the depths of a hollow
valley carved through the masses that teem
on this speck in our universe
tumbling in nether,
bound in a circle.

when I found this place a part of me left
behind the jumbles of watered
gray beards and slashing albatross eyes
a sense of being a part
apart from those who never
went to sea.

reaching out finding homes
in the memories of a warm lap
any lap
in turmoil over the needs of others who don't care
and just when you want to sleep
another eerie moan,
please.

WORKING NIGHT MUSIC

Sakonnet River, Rhode Island 1996

obscenity is the way a boat strings a laced line through a man's life,
talking in a little girl's voice
whispering suggestive things just before you can hear them
on the darkened side of the mud street
along the water's edge
swearing to give you aids
and you'd like it always
with a maid
-ish ring of knowing
all that is secret
of the things you can't dream of in walleyed
splendor
just beyond the harbor wall
in the darkness
on the wet, tasseled beach scrabble,
sucking pebbles in mumbled mouths
turning a tide fair with a caress
of slick white froth
waiting for the next john
to come along
hiding
desires in her cold ballast heart
best
kept to one's self.

THE FIRST STORM OF WINTER
Jamestown, Rhode Island 1972

depression
it roared through last night
singing the rigging
pressing us over against the dock
twanging lines
sucking us down into foul bags of nitrous slumber
collecting sins in drops of mucus on the overhead

staying too long is an art
never to be practiced
by smart ones
but I'm glad for the cold
gasping like a lunger in the trill morning
huddled in scraps of thin fabric against the wind
finding solace in no decision other than the one to take us south.

hard is fine
against the mahogany of a steaming warm bar serving Narragansett
as if a choice were more sin
sucking other's smoke
rubbing lipstick from a glass, wondering
watching ash trays fill
and wasting the crisp clean day hiding from judgement.

knowing the stream is out there
rolling in bricks
kicking the mules
breaking backs
keeps us hugging the wood slats
heaving in the inner harbor
hoping a high will finally take us.

streets are poor
cover
with no car to hide behind
no doors to open
no place to be
long
in.

SHOOTING THE COOK
Hobart, Tasmania 1973

mawing mouths are silent
as twenty work their way through dinner
passing the bowls goes without a word
gestures are given and in kind
grunts answer
pass the vegemite is the only
needed chorus.

cook goes on deck
to not see the toils of an afternoon's trials vanish with
smacking lips
and shuddering wordless neutrality,
no wonder
cooks are
notoriously low on attitude and selfless esteem.

the all hands
leaves plates cold as
creamed corn
swaying in the
gimbals
dead sentinels of another
watch break moving against fiddles.

food on land is a commodity
at sea
a liability
for ill feelings over helpings
over plates left half consumed
for resentment
and the pointed warm rush of broken tipped knives.

love all cooks
the least of which
fights the temptation to spit
in the soup of three squares
and leaven a disdain
of hawkish disregard for those
who sit and wait on deck.

V-BERTH BOOGIE
Nantucket, 1988

twice I shush her mute
third time's a charm
he's looking at me
she says in a staged scare whisper
he sleeps with his eyes open
I say.

since
like
when.

I shrug in the dark in my sweaty bunk.

stick him with a pin
she says
if he screams we'll
know,
faker boy
moron,
miscreant, freak show, her whispers.

I'd scream too, I offer

your point she asks with passion
gaping eyes deserve
trial by ordeal
guilty suffer, innocent survives boiling oil,
fire ants and honey
dunking.

popcorn test, I say to her squirming sister-like wickedness.

a jiffy later
faker boy got none
until he
could sleep
with his eyes
shut.

JOEL
The Seaman's Hall, New Bedford 1972

there is also, always
one crew
whose name (be, Poindexter, pluh-ease)
begins with a
soundless admonition
to be quiet.

BALLS OF COINS

Charlotte Amalie, St. Thomas 1978

walking the deck
dictating to us, every
where, what his profit of the day was
as a thousand jaws clenched tight around a cigar
on wall street
the bell rang.

on paper worth
the day would go
from bad to worse
radio squawks
nausea was his atmosphere
jingling the balls in his pockets with battered cold coins.

up and down razor thin beaches
trades blew
sun peppery
trees swayed in the bombast shade of spiteful memories
when his money came once each year in
the division of profits taken from tobacco pensions.

we were parted in ways bent in silent object
each knew the other only,
he was made for ports of calling
his sex the stuff of who he tried to be
each day he coughed it up, the juice of his life and
spat it in my ear.

take your self
he would say
and I would stop listening, staring beyond
the horizon too flat by far for
the height he needed
to stand above what he couldn't climb and would never understand.

DOLDRUMS

Equator, Atlantic, 2005

a Hopi
on the longest day of the year
stares at the sun
from dawn
to dark
his eyes forever.

so that his people
could see
the other worlds
in their chaos, shadows
mean spirited animal voices
and full of whispered torments for a blind man.

Mary Buffalo
Charlie Charcoal
peyote dreams
under coyote piss piccadilly
waves holding
the jungle of stationary kelp beds to bay.

hapless, lazy
like the last words
of a love affair
lanquishing on water
as supple as a glass of stout
loneliness and time, cloy
the two defining dimensions of any voyage.

blind and brain hazed
lost in dopey splendor
a random gurgles drools attention
spritz bubbles sledge aft in glacial time
eyes follow
freely
a familiar, faithful nothing.

CHOWDER

The Mud Hole, Great Wass Island, Maine 2003

bacon,
sizzles, spurts, splatters butterscotch counters
onions paired in julianed splendor
cut like crescent moons
thin spread on cast iron hell
opaque, a word for transition
texture, mush
'taters in skin chunked, bite size querulous jumble
join the fray to soak the pig fat
butter spooned
covered, undone, shameless peeking
half of this
half of prudent cream
bubbles through
slimy milk sticks under, feckless
wooden spatula loosens the heart stopping scum
of old bay salt, pepper, 'wooster sauce
celery flakes in feathers delivered
on cool wide bowls
and spoons licked
in stomach spasms
of the last drip
but one
and memories of others built for lugubrious reasons in cold rain on
long dark nights
riding to heavy air
in fifty plus of latitude
mumbles in oil lamp gold
sighs when the pot is half empty
tucked behind
crusty bread, cut unmoldy for palate toothed desert.

WHAT IS THE OCEAN?

Dedicated to Tristan Jones, dead, Nevis 1995

the ocean is a bottom, trenched in continental turmoil
barely known burials
of lightless orbital eyes
searching
for morsels from above
not knowing if it is dangerous, nourishment, life giving
putting the tasting first, beyond
all else, behind a good sea story,

it is salt and oil, trial, trouble
sad
stinging nettles
wide jaws and crusty claws
pushing the beginnings back,
before legs
lungs
hearts and pains crushed in depths of pleasure, pressure.

where does the love go
thoughts fly
when death comes
and we keep inside the sweaty sour smell
the crooked smiles when nothing else fits, why,
is this life so powerless, drab
and sickly sweet
to think it is all.

when I heard of the milk white ashes minus a leg or two
gone in a swirl
into the cold craven waters
the breath left me
at a hundred fathoms
freediving
unable to let go of the rock wrapped around my hands,

all sea stories are all true,
living large in a bottle
of spew, spume and specifics, haunted by small minds, never there
you just
remember them
differently
each
time.

the ocean is not ear petals of whales
tasting like
fever sucked knuckle bones
a warm heart of oak, seagull soup
Welsch orphans begging
truffles of dirt,
standing tall without gams for the rest of us
around a life filling a trench of wants.

San Blas Islands 2009

WAKING ON THE BEACH

Kingston, Jamaica 1969

waking on the beach, alone
cabanas, glaring in blue striped pain,
mouth of red river valley dust
tongue deviling my teeth
in sticky gulps
of morning air heaving
to sore enough ribs
and one eye gummed shut,

we won, a voice cautions against coma
why not, I croak, not bothering a memory, dismissing images of
fat cats in air splendor
conditioning fools to
expect cool folded twenties to appear
in pockets of shorts that hung
all days racing in the oily swells.

life hates a morning loser
except for all the rest
as crab footprints lead
away from my trampled face
to the mangrove world
in spidered
legs above my sweat molded bed.

a name twinkles on the horizon
mine
a buoy in the fog
of the night before
best spent
never again, while
a bow legged ant moves away with a spittle grained sand
building a new universe from what I left on the beach.

WATERSIDE

Valdez, Alaska 1992

I want to know
if the sea is sick we feel it,
if a life is sick we die,

floating death from container ships
suckles roaming turtles
to a killing bed,

careful cockles
winks and whelks, string lace on eggs, foam
freedom of the seas is not meant to pollute,

the seas are a global commons
trash yard of the poor
sewer of the rich,

no longer in
fine
it.

longer line kill more fish
loner cowboy, lastly ends meeting
fine for banks, Swiss oil.

stop, single, hulled, drunks
if the sea is sick we all die
panda pocked sorrow, now and forever

church bombed 'bama girls
in gingham, for world peace, is the lead story, spill second
don't we ever outlast, unlearn, solve
tar baby stories, mea culpa,
isn't it time?

SAIGON
Fort Lauderdale, 1974

mine eyes still see
helicopters dropping the last of our
grainy despair
in skinny figures with pressed white shirts
tight black pants, shower clogs
lost hopes, lies, broken bones.

embassy lines to the roof
behind razor wire
casting about
for a reason to be not alive, disappeared
as the black shirt peasants filed
from the bloody fields
to retake their homeland.

endless silent bars on the waterfront pit stops
pissing warm bear in stools
of loud mouths
closed in shameless consternation, stubborn imperialists
against the cheers in Berkley
and the snickers
from doves, black crows.

fucking McGovern hippies, he said
and slugged back a glass of beam, a bloated belly polishing the mahogany
it was April, spring, total toddy time
SORC and the duels of money machines finally
over, looking for one last reason to go home
I put my beer mug to his ear, so he could hear the coming tide of peace
it broke.

FIRST THE THUNDER
Solomons Island 1987

snaking vampire's kiss snuggles
up in the dark sky, humming
on the green hills where
wind belches blue Dutch with the smell
of hog's bowels
and then platinum lightning.

scrambles up deck and down
moving in the old movie
staccato images
of shattered
sleep and desire to get below
before.

smelling the lack of oxygen
like covers over your head
ozone snapping as masts sway
inviting the life ending slap
of bolts, running to the sea
sucking the hook crocodile's clock to your bunk side.

no pans
in a lightning storm, with
life measured in killiseconds
knowing if you hear
it
you have dodged the jones
once again.

DEAD MAN'S FLOAT
West Palm Beach 1994

north wind
against the blue stream
kicking up marching elephants
across the hoary path to Bimini.

doing the dead man's float
in the piss water warm pool, waiting, proofing
saggy calves drooping to puckered green feet
as the lungs pop in smackered joy with each slaving breath.

she dangles a loverly leg
lazing shark white
against my side
opening a vein of doubt,

that she believes silently, never I can not
swell it home,
find the hole
park it safe when the cold calamity story-lings in.

I curse the wind
fault the current, blame the boat,
pop a breath of mucus and saliva and sink
once again into one full atmosphere of uncertainty.

hardly worth the time
to imagine
a world, the next dead man's inhale,
without her calm hemorrhaging trust.

HOVE TO

Flemish Cap, North Atlantic 1991

canvas cocoon wedged tight
against the brutal attacks
on elbows, hips, knees
from any surface
varnished or rounded
not pillowed.

feeling like a broken promise
kept too long
smelling of soggy sweat
and fear that one watery
rumbling freight train will
turn us out inside.

thoughts pick away
words unsaid to a loved one
a kick to a defenseless dog
a slight, a cruel look
in the very ever,
your mother's face caught in a lie.

hours drag on
boat makes new noises
to test your imagination
of disasters
far worse than
you or anyone imagines.

always you open the hatch
just to see if it is as bad
as hell on steroids
it is
shaken, you wedge back in
to sleep with the hag of endless hope.

A WHOLE GALE
Puerto Rico Trench, 1982

no safety equipment piece can tell you
in lost hope of a fiftieth hour, as cold
reality scratches along the slate
that has nothing to do with azimuths, logarithms
shriekingly present, pinpoint accurate, a hat trick fix,
the end of all things.

noise
booming explosive concussive
ear-popping fifty caliber rattles, Krupa riffs
bone grinding death groans over endless
whelping thunder
in the lulls.

your insides move, entrails slop
as water and air, push and pull
tugging for and by torturing
rigging and accidental watchmates
inside out fifty times an hour
wedged to a soggen bunk.

nothing sleeps
everything breathes, rolls, shivers
no tragedy left unopened
last rites spoken, taken back
alone, fifty knots,
            all gales are whole at sea.

A SINGLE HAND

Dedicated to Jim Stanek, Bristol, England 2005

out of the Plume and Feather
Dicken Pretty
of Pictan Street
steam rolling in a norther
sat in baggy splendor
on Peggy's slopping keel.

missed the last night locks in a rage
of weathers
tied outside
the eight meter tide
she found a pile
to straddle down.

Howl Price and the lads of Bristol
foiled the bollixed turn
and tingled up the hole
in handle bar moustaches
under a single squirreled
brow.

steammate Stanek swoons
for Bunny Breedin's girl
and Major Martin Minterkamp
cuts the bonnie nupt cake at tan-A-farms
with a slash
of embroidered saber steel.

tea a three
root canal at lunch
arrofini, pasties, gum snappin birds
and whiskey currents
the color
of tired pence.

Scily
to think of this as our lost day, forsloppin'
to bray in the
tall rust of
hay ashore by Carrick Roads.

WINDWARD PASSAGE
Nassau, Bahamas 1971

a wind caress on water, pulling, kneading, single molecules at a time
waves begin to fetch
spew tendrils in row on row off swirling green gray beards
growing in mean spirited towers as the spit warm current tugs away the
    fathom deep foundations leaving airborne brick chimneys
spreaders frame bright white rumbling freight trains on a dark night
watch.

racing an addiction of poor choice and minimal reward
ripping up hundred dollar bills in a cold shower for days
shivering in catalytic tremors and scared of the very next second, all ways
out of control, with no rational response at the helm,
there was the sailing too.

Lauderdale to Nassau across the Bahama Banks
we ape trimmed and rode the weather rail while the waves came up and
over
our boots full of wet wool and ball shivering testosterone
a single thought without a voice as wind and wave become solid over the
bow.

we slow her down now, right now
or we die with water in our lungs
I scream into the howl and spray, giddy about booming out
the number one for more,
the return look from the watch captain is a man gut shot.

hanging on with my feet dangling I feel her before the reality hits
we slide down a wave, black watery walls grow to fifteen feet
above, behind, a sound of the ocean splitting open, a red copper anvil
driven by
    a balloon of red white and blue
Windward Passage roars by with her spinnaker straining the laws of
probability
eighteen knots and she was gone before our pucker's sphinctered out
she won,
we played to a tie,
the halcyon days screeched on in helter-skelter scurry.

THE WRECKING TREE

Green Turtle Cay, Abaco 2005

fishing never works
out so well
for the bait
under big troubled skies
in tiki bars
on stumbled down docks.

black curls bookend
the saddest face
on da place,
lips puffed in a wound
eyes bleaker than squid ink,
serious tits.

he came on
in easy cloudy grace
eyes veiled, mouth open
words as noxious
as a rattling halyard
pushing the line
mashing the gas.

teeth white
eyes roll
she bite back.

Ondine off Mexico 1974

Roque Island 2019

ABOUT THE AUTHOR

R. J. Rubadeau has crisscrossed the globe under sail. A licensed captain with a hundred-ton master ticket for all oceans, he has logged well over two hundred and fifty thousand miles in boats ranging from Olympic class skiffs to maxi-ocean racers. His family's yacht, *Dog Star*, is an eighty-nine-year-old wooden classic kept in near Bristol condition in the vessel's home waters in Maine.

An award-winning poet, author, novelist, professional speech writer, and political consultant with a long publication resume of fiction, poetry and non-fiction, R. J. Rubadeau was the 2004 recipient of the Mark Fischer Literary Prize for Poetry. These are poems gathered from publications, logbooks, and journals spanning fifty years of experiences fraught with the challenges and vagaries of life at sea in small boats.

The decades from 1968 until the turn of the century are often called the Modern Classic Age of Sail with Dennis Connor, Warren Brown, Ted Turner, Ted Hood, Chay Blyth, Carlton Mitchell, Sir Peter Blake, Tristan Jones, Bernard Moitessier and the hundreds of other colorful icons of the sailing world providing the fertile ground for an exploration of sailors and the sea. The author has sailed with, among, for, and against them all.

This is a collection of insights, visions, and observations intended for the armchair sailor in all of us. These distilled celebrations of life at sea are best enjoyed read aloud in some quiet little anchorage illuminated by an oil lamp, bobbing gently to your own hook.

From the tropical equator to the arctic coasts of the Bering Sea, from the islands of the Caribbean to the tip of Cape Horn, from Tasmania to the Sea of Cortez, these epic sea stories in poems draw from the fear, discomfort, and uncertainty of putting to sea in fragile craft. Tight slices of experience celebrate the challenges, solitude, and joy of late-night watches while finally bringing a boat home with the voyage accomplished. This volume is a true celebration of a life spent under a spread of sail.

R. J. Rubadeau lives with his wife Mary and a posse of dogs, outlaw friends and horses in Durango, Colorado. Each summer, *Dog Star* plies the cold, clear waters of New England and beyond, crewed by hardcore shipmates and four generations of this seafaring family including Skye, Tristan, Allie, Maddie, Merrick, Macy, Summer, Robert (Captain), Libby and Ryder.

Ed.

www.ingramcontent.com/pod-product-compliance
Lightning Source LLC
Chambersburg PA
CBHW031313060726
47590CB00003B/1199

9780981731339